FIRSTMATTERPRESS

Portland, Ore.

THE DYING ROOM

THE DYING ROOM

annemarie eayrs

FIRSTMATTERPRESS

Portland, Ore.

First Edition

Published in the United States
by First Matter Press
Portland, Oregon

Paperback ISBN-13: 978-1-958600-12-2
Library of Congress Control Number: 2025945031

Editor: Hailey Spencer
Contributing Editors: Lauren Paredes, Emily Moon & ash good
In Cohort: nawa angel a.h., Violeta Garza & Claudia Saleeby Savage
Contributing Readers: Sonya Wohletz & Andra Vltavín
Copy Editor: Andra Vltavín

Cover: *The Dying Room* (ink/digital)
Copyright © 2025 by Pearlyn Tan
pearlyn.net

Book design by ash good
ashgood.com

This project was made possible by Regional Arts and Culture Council,
Multnomah County Cultural Coalition and Oregon Cultural Trust.

For my mothers

After hours of intense labor, the woman held her baby in the halo of her touch for a single moment. The woman could not let herself bond even though the small moon of her daughter's face peered up in a crying mirror of her own likeness. The baby's face was a perfect blend of the father's features and her own—his nose and her thin whisper of lashes. The next day, she bundled her daughter in a blanket and left her at the police station where she would be found quickly.

She left a note pinned carefully to the blanket with a name and a short message. The name was her grandmother's, and the message reminded the baby she would have a better life. She would be loved. She would not be forgotten.

I have seen worse sights than this

god tied my hands
the day I was born,
bound my wrists in thread
cutting, red, that spooled itself
around my arms
and caught me by the neck

the thread pulled me, ankles skimming
across the pacific, wet and waiting
to cornfields, buried me full
like a seed, but I didn't
make a sound

thread can bind
fate overrides
chance, lets orphans
claim kinship and the kind of love
that can only be bought
I was bought,

and my price hangs heavy
around my neck, grazes
my collarbone and chafes
against my heart
it cannot be sold,

though I would sell my thread
for pennies, set myself loose
in faraway cities
rather than be pulled
slow and indifferent
back to the earth
unraveled

Nobody

there is a fascination with orphans—babies left on doorsteps, swaddled in blankets and clean, untouched by history; children, wild with foreign and untamable blood; a battleground between nature and nurture, played out among the notches in her spine.

when the orphan is adopted, she is lifted to the status of adoptee. she is a gift; she is a blessing. she has been gifted; she has been blessed. her gratitude erects the four walls of her new home but does not fill the gaps between her bones, which are never quite bridged. her ribs remain orphaned.

the orphan reads these books, learns her role. she learns the adoptee is always malleable, always pure, always resilient. most of all, the adoptee is redeemable; she assimilates seamlessly. perhaps because the adoptee writes herself using whatever materials she is given, scrounges around for pieces with which to stitch herself together, to sew her vertebrae, finally, into one.

Or:

The woman looked down at the new baby in her arms, screaming, squirming, purple and red. Black tufts of hair stayed plastered to the child's soft scalp, not yet fused into one. Its whole body felt sticky and wanting. Needy and hot.

The woman placed the tiny mouth to her breast, but the baby's fists swung, hard, back and forth, and she would not latch. The woman silently pleaded with the child—this should be easy. This should be easier. Something about this should be good, should be love.

Maybe if the child had fed. Maybe if the child had slept those first few hours. Maybe if the child had looked more like its mother. Maybe if it had opened her eyes and smiled. Maybe.

there is no people without a nation

but here we are   displaced   and scattered
                                                along the edges
                                                of an unfamiliar
                                                plane

we are the nation's currency
        we trade ourselves   our bartered bodies
        born poor with more to lose   and none to give   but fingernails
                                                                the waxy substance
                                                                of our skin

our nation's anthem
        hummed to the beat   of shaking cribs   and whistled
                                                                into the shell
                                                                of a baby's
                                                                half-deaf ear

our nation's flag
        made of silk so soft   our fingers bleed   when we cling
        sewing   our own resilience
                                                                we hold ourselves
                                                                instead

prayers slip onto our tongues some days
roll out   of marble-stiff mouths   parched with unspeaking
        until the words lodge   behind unfit lips   and will not come out

they tell me I have lost

a homeland, a culture, a family.
the word *abduction* is used

to displace my loyalties and hinges
on my bedroom door.
I do not feel

this loss when I open the door
of the fridge at two a.m. to the cool
bright pool of appetite at my feet, while I dig

past molding oranges
and unsealed bags
of lettuce, but rather

I feel loss when I read
of loss, when academics
write down my price,

cite my peers, cite myself to prove
scientifically
the hole in my being,

and I feel loss when I hear
of loss, when others
like me mourn past lives

and things that might have been,
when loss turns to anger
that can find no clear direction.

night swallows
the rest of the world and leaves me
floating, or perhaps night

swallows me
while the rest of the world
goes on living in color.

I can feel the tones of black
and white seep into the sockets
of my own dappled skin

but still I float, my bed adrift
in the fissure between continents
while I search for a diagnosis—

a ten-syllable fence for my heart
and its restless beating.

the nature of love

when given the choice
of food or cloth, harlow's monkeys
chose cloth every time; the scientists
thought they would choose the food,
which shows less about the monkeys
than how little we understand

the poor monkeys
raised with mothers of wire
had no place to run
when confronted with a beating
drum, a bear; they threw themselves down
clutching their faces—imagine
seeing a baby unable to find comfort,
a monkey that can only rock
and scream

when deprived of love
some monkeys could not eat,
as if they never developed
the ability to absorb, the hierarchy of needs
turned on its head
all for the feeling of cloth

we all belong to harlow,
revert to our infant selves—

we long for the ancient hum
of our mothers, the touch
of their hair. deprivation
leaves our bones hollow
and wanting; we cannot attach,
though she becomes fond
of the bite of my shoulder, and I will soon beg
for the press of her hands

Or:

*The woman hurriedly swaddled the baby, her fingers shaking. A small
noise from the next room made her pause, ears straining. Her family
must not catch her now. The woman picked up the baby who, blessedly,
shifted but continued to sleep in silence. The small movement made
the woman's heart tighten. The child slept without knowing what
disastrous luck it had to be born a girl. With the child in her arms, the
woman slipped out into the night.*

*Without being seen, the woman made it to the police station where she
deposited the child on a step near the black grate that would soon fill
with bicycles once the day broke. The concrete walls stood hard and
unforgiving, even as the small baby was placed within their arms. The
entrance to the compound loomed overhead. The woman could not
leave a note for fear it would be too easily traced back to her. The baby
began to wake, and the woman ran. This is not the end, she thought to
herself. Soon, she knew, they would try again, and hopefully her next
child would have the luck to be born a boy.*

the dying room

how did I escape
the dying room

the rows of cribs
ghost silent to haunt
my desk chair
that creaks its own
cries, not unlike them
the hundreds
of them, the thousands
the millions, stuck in the orphanage
still in my mind, my chair
that rocks to self-soothe
that rocks itself to heaven

the room lurks dark
in my memory, a leaking faucet
of my own demise; the documentary
tells us many orphans went
to die in those rooms
the government denies
what cameras have seen
the rooms are almost worse
for being bare

it's strange to find yourself
rare, an escape artist at two

days, then six months
there's a space inside my head
for sighing
and one gap between my teeth
for whistled prayer

my feet rock, too
my very soles
roll back and forth
I can't stand still
my big toe itches
to escape and longs
to take me with it

I cannot escape the dying
room, cannot

walk into walmart without my skin
crawling with tiny fingers
soiled with milk. I dream of needles
unpinned in scalps
whenever I smell lilacs

distended bodies
fill my arms and my thoughts

my hands are too small
with never enough blankets
my legs wear through
sheets, I'm always buying sheets
and running at night, from or toward
I do not know, but I put in miles
they put in more

I didn't think abandonment
followed me—I was so young
I didn't know the word
I didn't
know I had been left, but maybe
it does, maybe
abandonment echoes my movements
like the shadow of a printed word
perhaps it's easier
to pin my faults there
there, maybe
I was abandoned

and maybe today I exist
a living nature
nurtured into being
with movies, my script was given to me
young, I learned my lines
auditioned with a single photo

bald but young
my youth saved me
a month's difference
ruined another

she would have played the clarinet
and screamed less
instead of writing poetry
until my throat hurts and
the music is spent

I am told I do not act
like an only child, you cannot smell
a single board game on me, but
I'm not an only child
I'm sure I have a chinese brother
perhaps illegal sisters, kept instead
and raised
in a life so unfamiliar
it took me twenty years to recognize

I was a middle child
once. I am a middle child
still

some things just stick

what would I be
without the dying

room for improvement
always, but
I am neither political
nor correct, I tip-toe
along hyphens—
my gratitude, too
walks a fine line
inches from skeptical
they say I was saved

I am ungraceful and full
of ideas that lead me
in circles and circles
my mind churns into sea-
foam spoiling in my hands
when I try
and pin it down

I am ungrateful—we know it
gratitude runs circles
around my mouth, unrequited

it loves
to give and melt, it's never
fully honest with me
pining after hopes and hands
that hold and cradle thumbs
as spasms of terror
bind them

they bind me, my own mind
bides its time—to what
end, I devour
perhaps but feast alone
on wishes that unstay me

if I were to die
in this moment
hand to my chest in prayer
or pain, my things
would be given away
shirts packed and boxed
with shoes, fake diamonds
sewn to imitation leather
small hands stitching lines
that made me so happy
so guilty to buy

I would haunt
the living room
with unquiet noise
finally settle
between cushions
or under the rug
and it would serve me right
to ever have thought
I deserved such beautiful things

wash me white
wash me white
wash me

why
do I have to count pennies
I'm so sick
of counting pennies
and having people assume
that I don't, I'm sick
of worrying that I will die
homeless or lose
my car, I'm sick
of counting the days

how did I escape
the dying room

I will crawl back to it
on all fours, I will sing
my own lullabies
of death and decay and wilt
in the sweet petals
of my own shame
how did I ever
escape, why did I
deserve to escape, I wish
that I could go back
sometimes, I wish
I could go back
to that lone crib
waltz to the drumming
beat my bones
into china

I can't keep anything in my head
but fantasies, stupid, slow
mind bending
fastidiously toward unmixed
things, there's nothing in my mind
but shame, I can't look at myself
anymore

the room crowds behind
my eyes, it must reveal
through black pupils a single
bed, barren, broken
laden with a child, not me
but seen
through my eyes

I have a compulsion to crack
fortune cookies
split them in two, still
in the wrapper, the fortune visible
without ever being touched

every fortune tells me
I have lost my mother's face

this world was not meant for me
I want to

find myself
in the dying room
and that impossibly small girl
in my house, in my bed
cracking beneath the pressure
of a world not meant
for her

Or:

The woman let herself cradle her daughter for a second before passing the small body to her husband who quickly placed a rag over the newborn's mouth to stifle any cries that might give them away. He wrapped her quickly in a thin jacket, cast off from his first child, a son.

It had just turned into the first light of the morning as the man walked toward the edge of town. He passed the steps of a bakery and slowed to a stop. He had seen the woman who ran the shop sweeping in the mornings and knew she would be out soon. She would find the baby quickly, but she had also seen his face, watching. She might remember his eyes or his coat and suspect. The worry was enough to move him on until he approached the police station. It was quiet, and before he could talk himself out of it, he left his daughter on the station steps and walked back into the blooming day.

the ability to hear a note for what it is

escapes me, the songs all sound the same
to my ignorant ears while music
finer, thinner, flies
out of range.

when I was younger
I could hear the overtones
of laughter sparked by chords
of grief, my intuition caught lullabies
once, and they held.

my voice stays level, now
it flatlines when I yell
or whisper love; love is entitled
to a language with notes
my adopted tongue has none
but beats that align
with my heart sometimes
and tick away my thoughts.

deafness will reach me
in my age and isolation, I am told
I must go on living, all the while knowing
there is a certain music
I will never hear.

double vision

how does it feel to be a problem?
I will tell you, I feel unwhole,
unholy and brown.
let me tell you how it feels to be saved:
borne out of white guilt and doubled,
born running and kept
running away from myself, toward my own reflection;
I chase ghosts who care nothing for me and scorn
my dissatisfaction; my skin betrays me
and warns other children away,
lets them know that this one
is not to be trusted, always running, fed
but still hungry with ingratitude.
my neighbor's daughter lived in china;
she couldn't breathe, choked by the smog, and she tells me
every day, describes the very hold it took
on her lungs; her mother describes it, too, complains to me
of my people. I wait in line at the grocery store;
my mother had eggs and milk to buy, and I
held the bread and waited; we stepped up to the counter together;
I placed the bread by the scanner; *excuse me, ma'am,*
this woman was next. he gestures to my mother, doesn't realize we
are together; to be separated so easily, our kinship divided
on a conveyor belt, plastic guillotine, easier
than holding hands, I forget our love is not as visible
as matching blue eyes or the same blonde hair, my hair,
black and unyielding, untidy as I am, a problem,
I, a problem

Of all creatures

my body writes illegibly
it cannot hold
a pen, cannot

                                 read the future etched
                                 in its own well-traversed
                                 palms

my face remains foreign
even
to itself

                                 in the way that lanterns
                                 hang in gardens and make a place
                                 feel far away

I forget my face, sometimes,
mirrors recall the shape
of my eyes

                                 the sliver of dark lashes, hair
                                 like mine, eyes like
                                 mine, skin

my heart is one, self-divided
flesh, it is the third lobe
of my lung—

                                 it, too, must breathe.

white cheddar

the plastic bag
nicks my wrist, leaves powdered cheese,
already festering and yellow
with salt

I find myself
on the nutrition table
between *percent* and *value,*

after natural skin the color
of burnt rice
and the oriental flavor
packets in twelve-cent ramen,

but not in the rice cake itself,
white as god's face
or the tender inside of a
crab rangoon

Or, maybe:

*The child cried out, perhaps from hunger. The older woman began
to rock the baby, just enough to soothe its immediate distress into
murmurs. This baby's mother—just a girl, really—would not miss it, the
older woman was sure. The girl was fifteen, too young to be a mother
and unmarried on top of it all. Yes, this was better for the mother and
the child both.*

*The mother may have given the baby up for adoption anyway, left the
struggling bundle at a police station for hard hands to find. A good
story, the woman decided. And this way the baby would find a home
in America, she told herself, and at least someone would make some
money from the deal.*

witch'd

I rub the wildness of it against my teeth, gleaming
in its own light and fierce, running my tongue
along its knife edge, the beating iron core of it
the steel of my nails, the flint
of my bones; it's then that I know of exactly what
I am capable. I know of the fires

I would light, the heat of them; I'd watch
it burn, I know to what depths
I would go, just give me an hour
to dream, not of the beast
of me, that hairy face, and rough and wild,
but something different
nameless and sweet

what do they know
of me, my power, my killing words, what lies
beside me at night; the great
and tawny lioness prowls
my hours and days, my wicked spells,
her violent eyes; it's me, she sees—

a bloodied maw,
my many-toothed heart,

I would, it beats,
I would
I would

revised

so I can ask, finally,
why the world is always ready for your kind of hate
but never mine?

—from "Vu Nguyên's Revenge" by Bao Phi

books fill with the faces,
the same faces you see
on money; my wealth
is not measured
the way you measure yours,
not in accomplishment
and worth but in product; I supply
what you demand

and exhaust myself learning,
educating myself of my own past lives,
own history; you will not find me
in textbooks, in the curriculum
standardized, sanitized
out of my brown hands,
I could not find myself,

though I looked for years
among white faces, straight
faces, male
faces open books
to see themselves—

I can't find myself.
I had to write myself.

I live censored
and on the brink
of silence, imposed
by my own desire
to please;
my silence sells

when I write,
the back of my mind fills
with my mother.
I write for her, or rather
it is for her sake that I pick and choose
which parts of myself
to share and which parts of myself
I will allow to stay

for her I dilute my anger,
try my best to heat it and blow
it to something worth keeping,
displayed in the window
where neighbors can see
and comment
on its tranquility

I live complicit, planted yellow,
I was grown
wholesome and quiet
in a white field where
my anger feels like declaring war
on those I love instead of declaring love
for those at war

There is a time for many words

i.

I left at eight months, too young
to remember, thrust onto the sea;
I dreamed of returning, of hair that matched mine
and flowering trees and slipping into a crowd
unnoticed. What teenager wouldn't dream
of going unnoticed. I imagined eating soups
my tongue would know and hearing a song
that would fit into the tightly curled cave of my ear.

I wished to be Odysseus, come home
after ten years of sailing, unmoored and afloat,
to slip back to belonging and hailed
as a king, to be known by my scars,
the history of my body unchanged
over years and the lines of my palm
a bridge to past lives.

ii.

Part monster, part man,
the bridge could barely hold him;
the weight of his companion
pulled at his elbow and guided him
along the rough stones; his eyes

were missing, but he could see
the way a bat sees, the echoes of pity
bouncing off strangers,
skimming the hairs on my forearms
and blowing away.

The smell of raw sewage plumed up
from the river below, and I wondered
if the smell was worse for him
in his blindness

I return to him in my dreams
the man on the bridge, the man
with no eyes;
when I return, sometimes,
I put a few heavy coins in his cup;
sometimes I wash his feet with my hair,
and when the sun rises, I wake
and dream of unseeing,
of pushing past a sea of strangers
I cannot fathom,

of lotus blossoms
falling into polluted rivers

iii.

I fear that lotus blossoms help me forget
my home, make me complacent
with time-worn images and silk screen
shadows—the true webs
get lost in pearls, slipped out of shells
with the slick of a knife and scraped into dust
to illustrate worth

I am a pearl myself, I know that knife,
that double edge; it chafes at my skin
and the others beside me, it scares me
into remembering
when I only wish to sleep

Maybe:

The worst part of it all is that she was loved. That she was wanted.
But that she was still given away and that now she would never know.

afterword

In 1995—the year I was adopted—a documentary team led by reporters Kate Blewett and Brian Woods traveled to China to visit orphanages to prove the existence of "dying rooms," rooms where orphans were left to die of neglect. Orphanages were struggling to handle the heavy influx of abandoned babies due to China's One-Child Policy, and rumors had begun to swirl that babies who were sick or disabled were being left in rooms without care until they passed.

Blewett and Woods used hidden cameras to capture footage, documenting babies tied to beds, strapped to potty chairs, and languishing in barren cribs. No definitive footage was taken of a dying room, but the film shocked the world nonetheless.

There have been rebuttals to their film, *The Dying Rooms*, claims that what they captured was exaggerated and without substance. But it was too late: the world had seen, truthful or not, a story so disturbing that it would spur many, including my own mother, to adopt a child from China, to save a child from the unthinkable fate of a dying room.

After watching the documentary for the first time when I was seventeen, I felt grief, of course, horror, naturally. And relief. I finally had a name for the shadow lurking at the back of my mind. For years she had no name, just a weight, but at last I stood with her face to face: she is the dying.

ANNEMARIE EAYRS is a writer and transracial adoptee from China who writes words she wishes she had when she was young. Raised in Minnesota, she now lives with her wife and their many pets in SE Portland.

2025
FEATURED ARTIST PEARLYN TAN

WALING WALING PALPITATIONS
nawa angel a.h.

THE DYING ROOM
RECIPIENT OF THE PRIMA MATERIA AWARD
annemarie eayrs

BRAVA
violeta garza

FIRST YOU MUST DESTROY THE WORLD
claudia saleeby savage

2024
FEATURED ARTIST ALEXANDRA STRENFEL

GREENHOUSE
sophie hall

SUSPENDED IN MY INSECTICIDE JAR
clara mcauley

2023
FEATURED ARTIST LARA ROUSE

FLOATING BONES
rae diamond

TEN-CENT FLOWER & OTHER TERRITORIES
charity e. yoro

OUR FAVORITE PEOPLE IN THE ROOM
edited by ash good, lauren paredes & emily moon

2022
FEATURED ARTIST RACHEL MULDER

BETWEEN THESE BORDERS WANDERS A GOLEM
ahuva s. zaslavsky

EVEN THE AIR, TOO HEAVY
riley danvers

ONE ROW AFTER / BIR SIRA SONRA
sonya wohletz

SOMEONE I CAN HOLD GENTLY
xylophone mykland

STORIES FOR WHEN THE WOLVES ARRIVE
hailey spencer

2021

2020

2019

2018

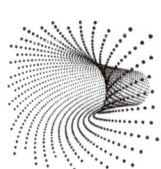

FIRSTMATTERPRESS
Portland, Ore.

www.ingramcontent.com/pod-product-compliance
Lightning Source LLC
Chambersburg PA
CBHW051336120626
46547CB00016B/2568